Alphabet Apple Tree

Trace the letters and color the tree.

1

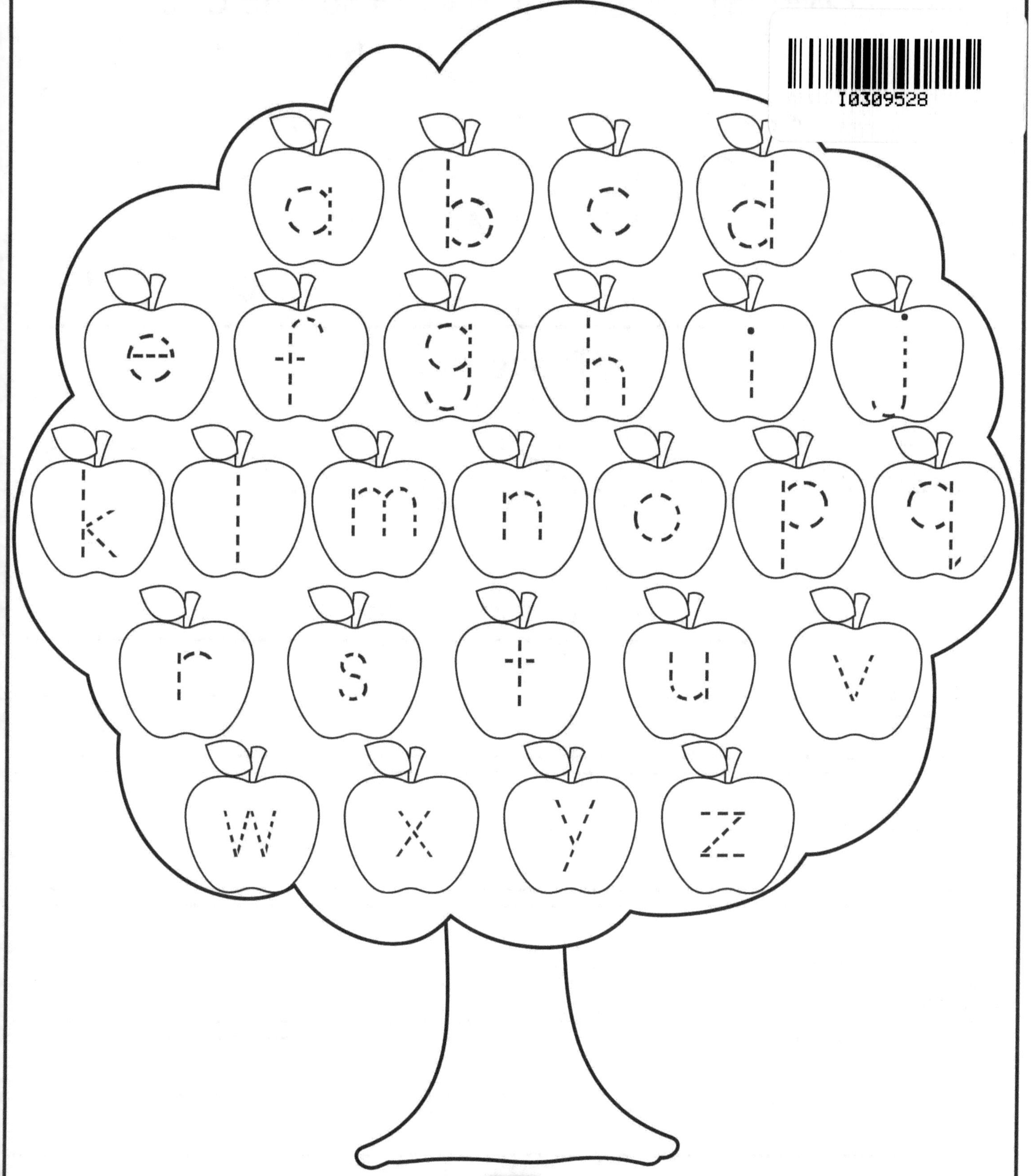

Alphabet

Color it!
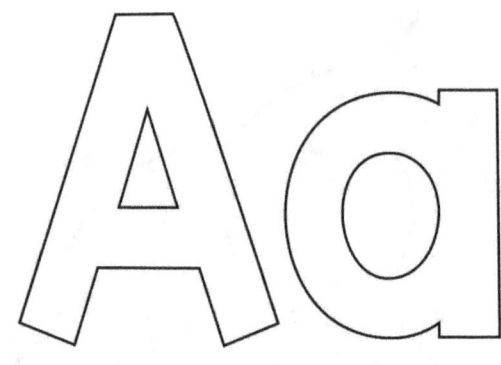

Find and Circle
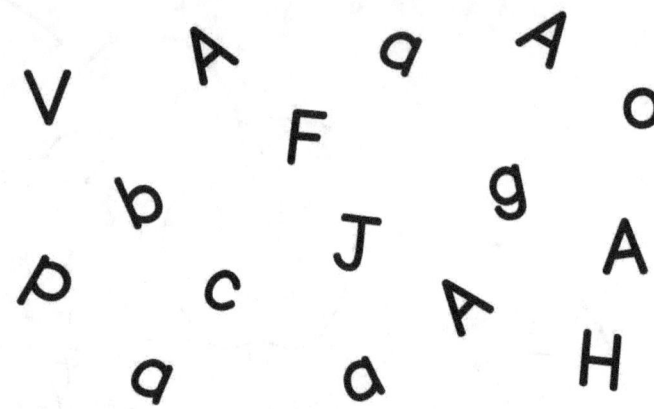

Trace it!

apple

Trace and Write

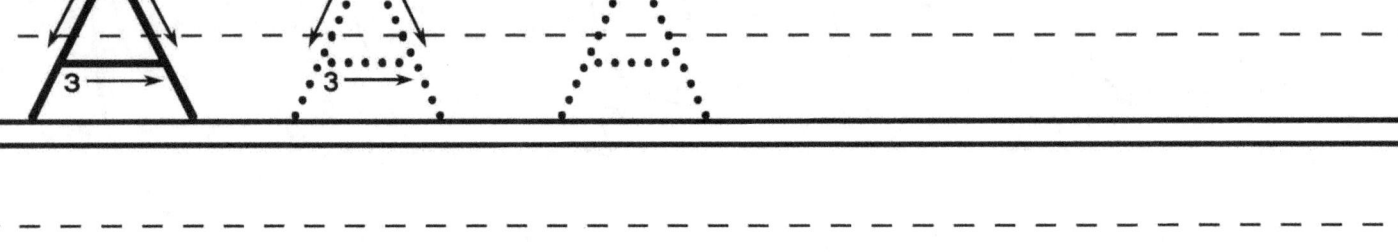

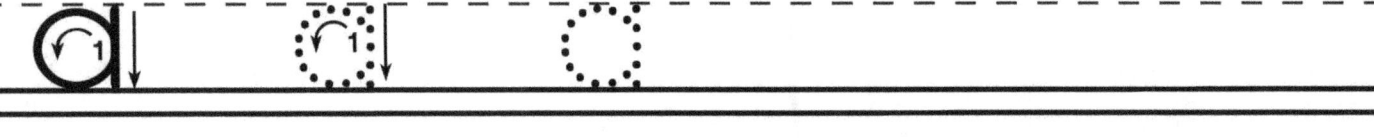

2

Find The Letter

Trace the letter and color the circles that have "A".

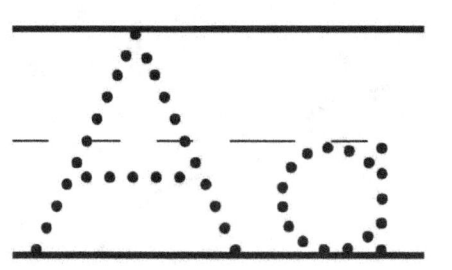

Aa is for Apple

S J a B
a A A
A V T G
E I a k
a A X A
U

Apple Tree Shapes

Color the apples by their shapes.

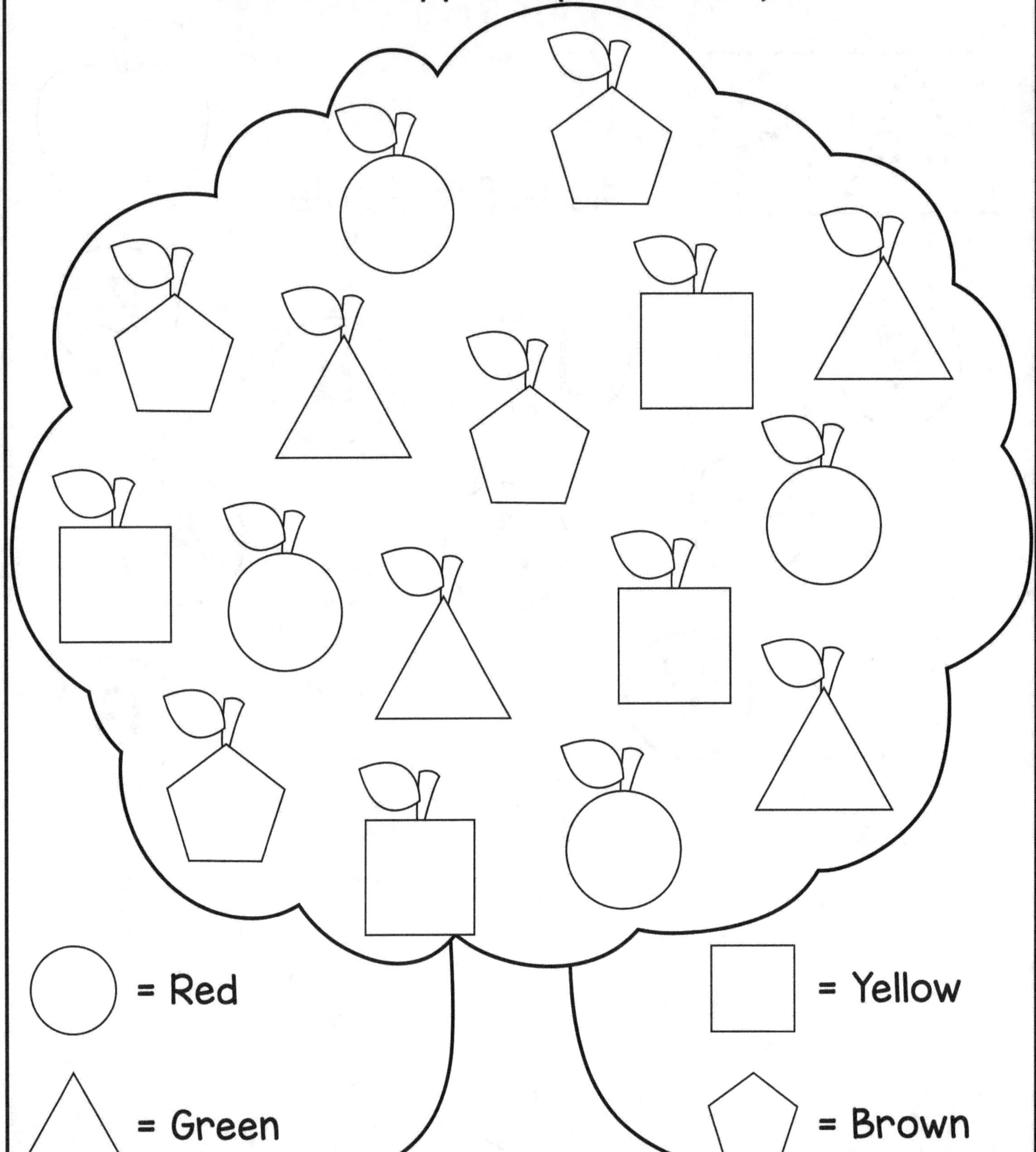

◯ = Red   ☐ = Yellow

△ = Green   ⬠ = Brown

4

Apple Tree Sequencing

Color, cut and paste the pictures in order.

1	2	3
4		5

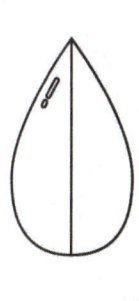
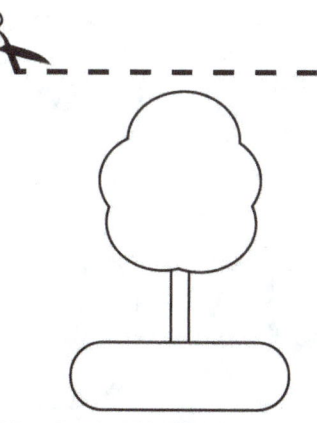
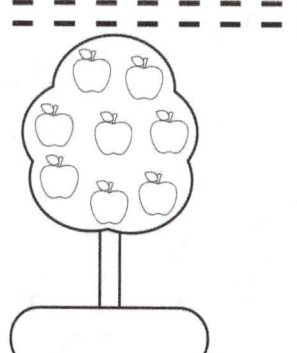

Find The Letter

Find and color the circle with pink having letter "A" and color the circle with orange having letter "a".

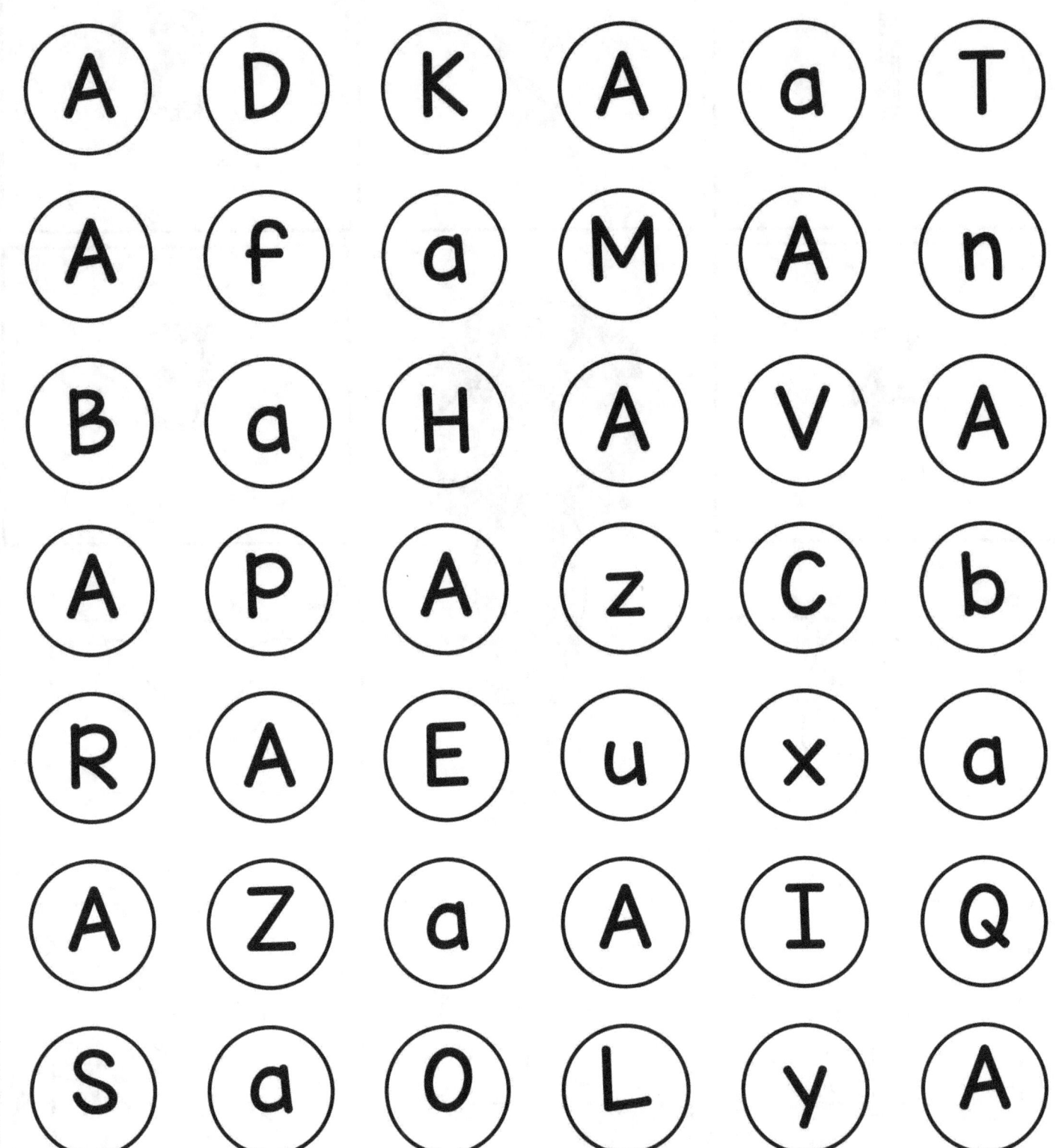

Label The Apple Tree

Cut and paste the words to label the apple tree. Color the apple tree.

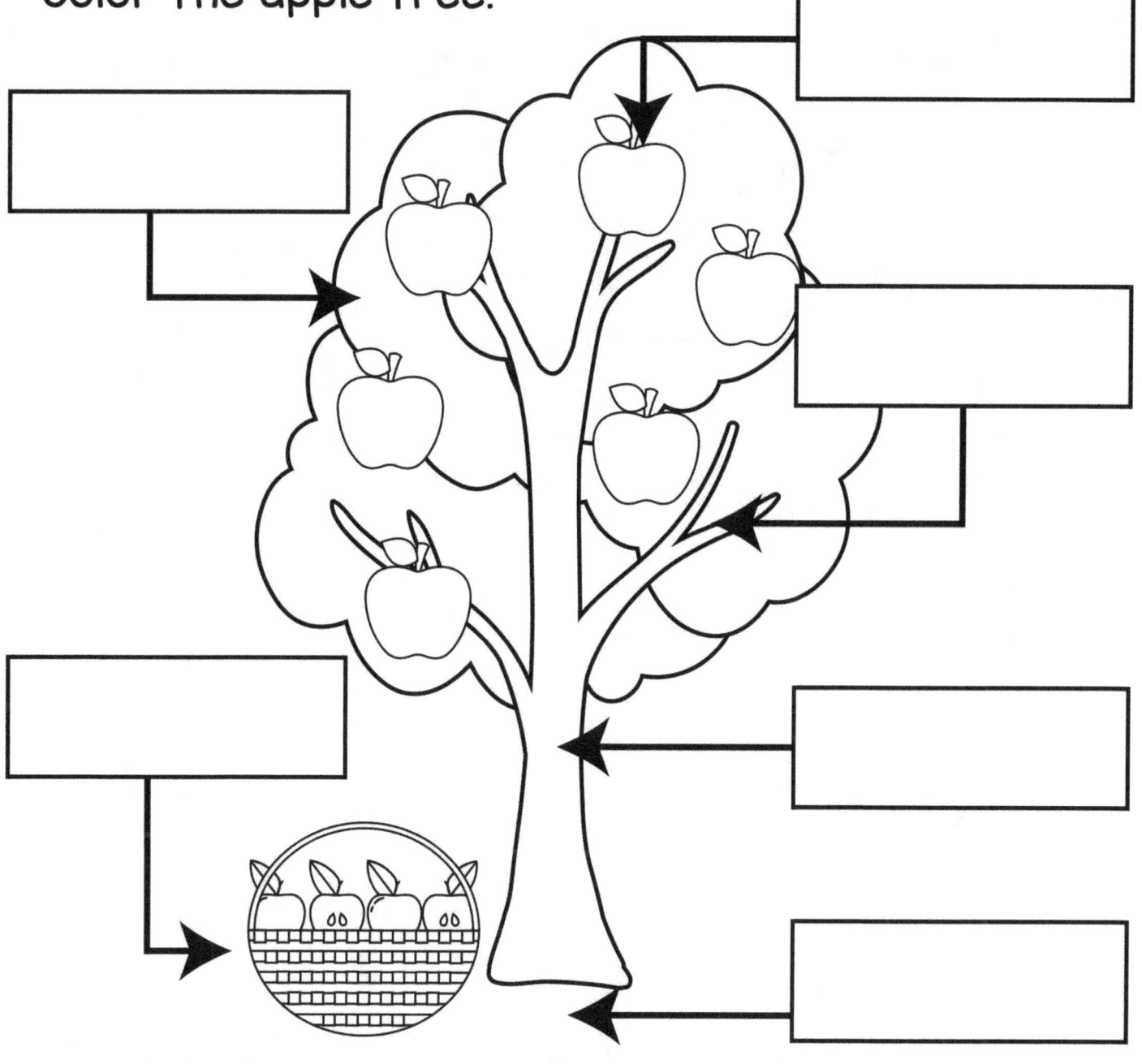

| apple | leaves | trunk |
| roots | branch | basket |

Color The Apple

Color the apple as shown in the picture.

Match The Letters

Cut and paste the letters on the correct apple.

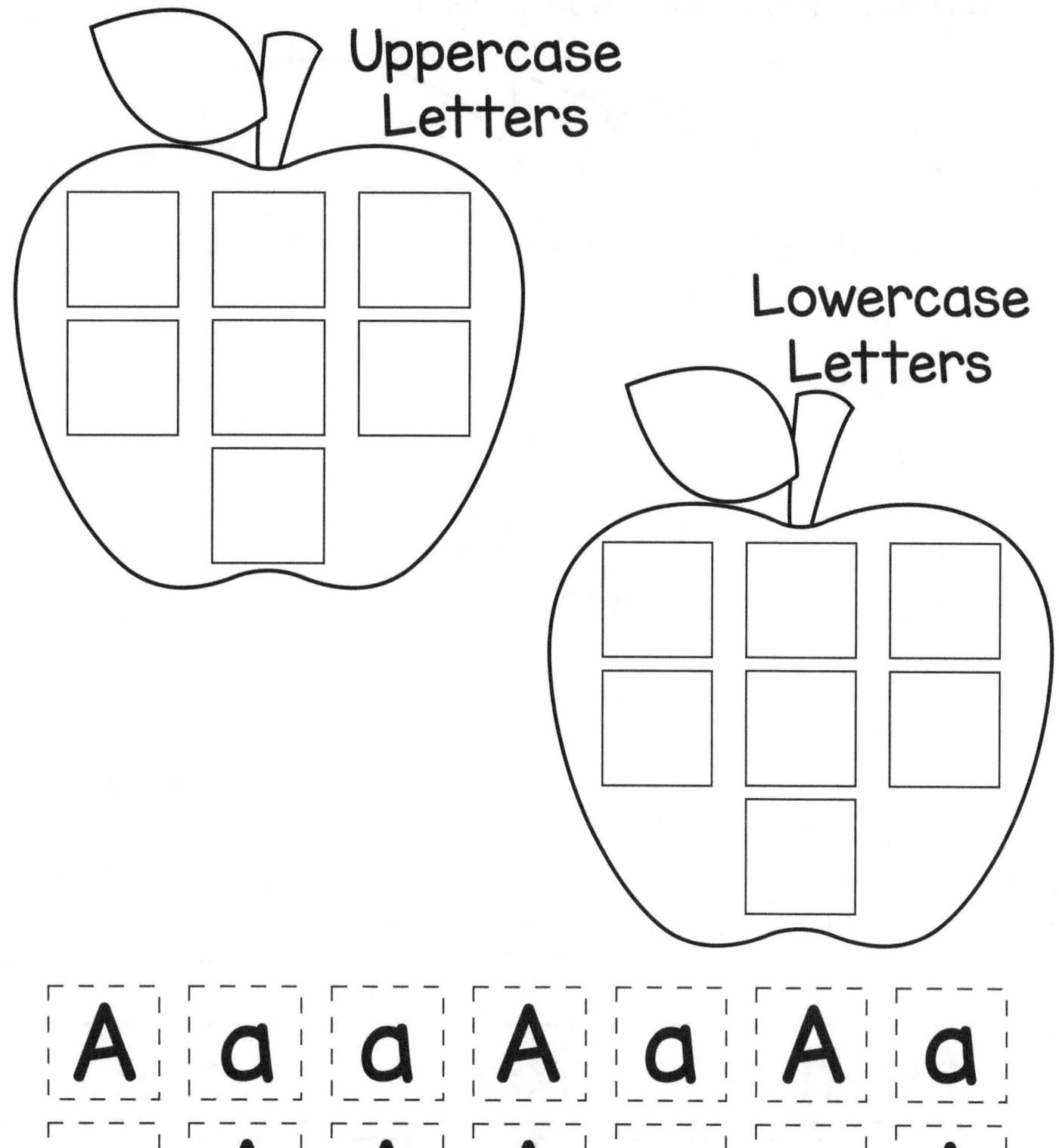

Label The Parts Of The Apple

Write the words from below to label the parts of the apple and color the apple.

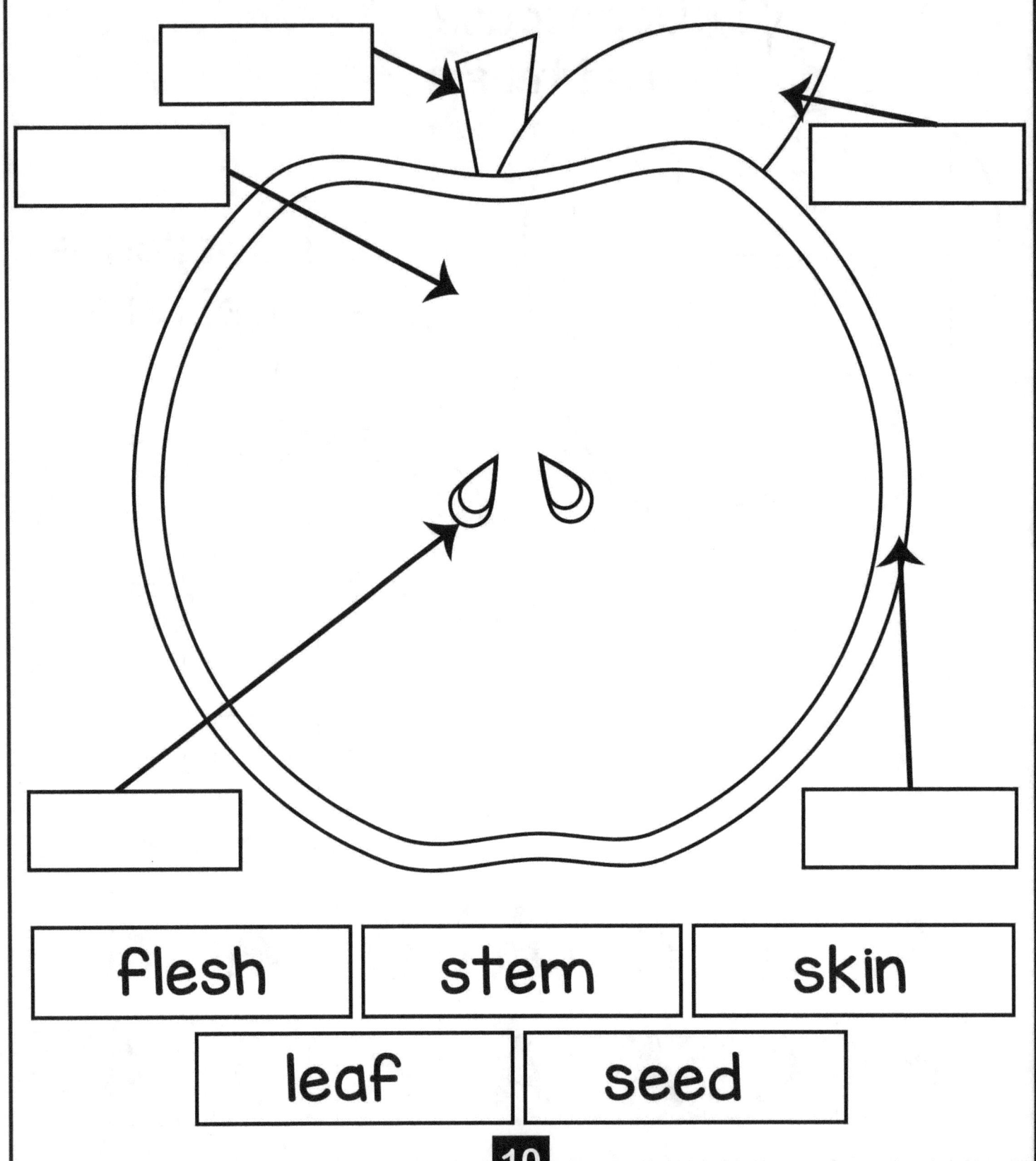

| flesh | stem | skin |

| leaf | seed |

Apple Pattern

Cut and paste the image below to complete the pattern and color it.

Apple Dot To Dot

Connect the dots to complete the picture and color it.

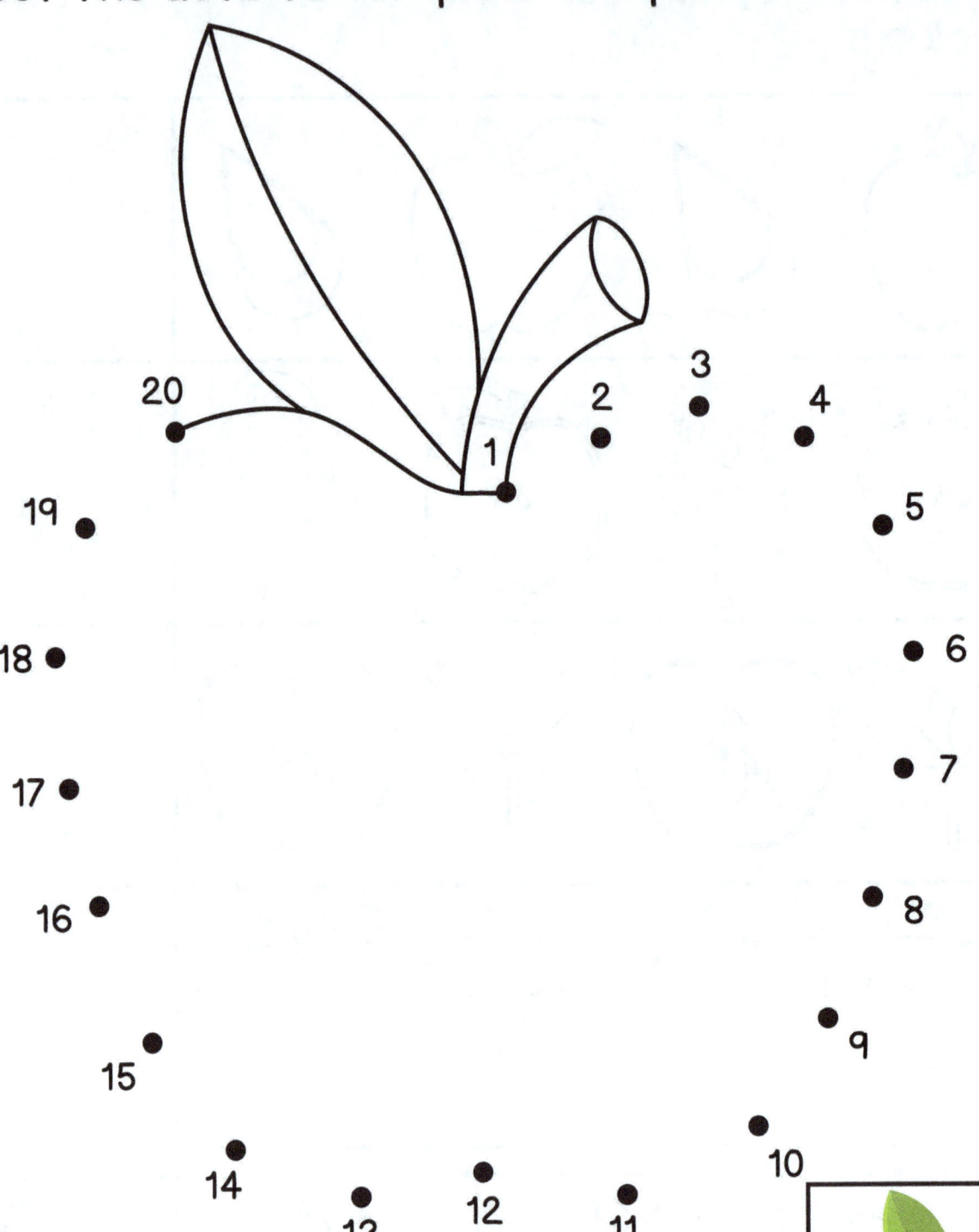

Apple Counting

Cut and paste the apple in the correct basket.

Apple Ten Frames

Fill in the ten frames to match the numbers on the apple.

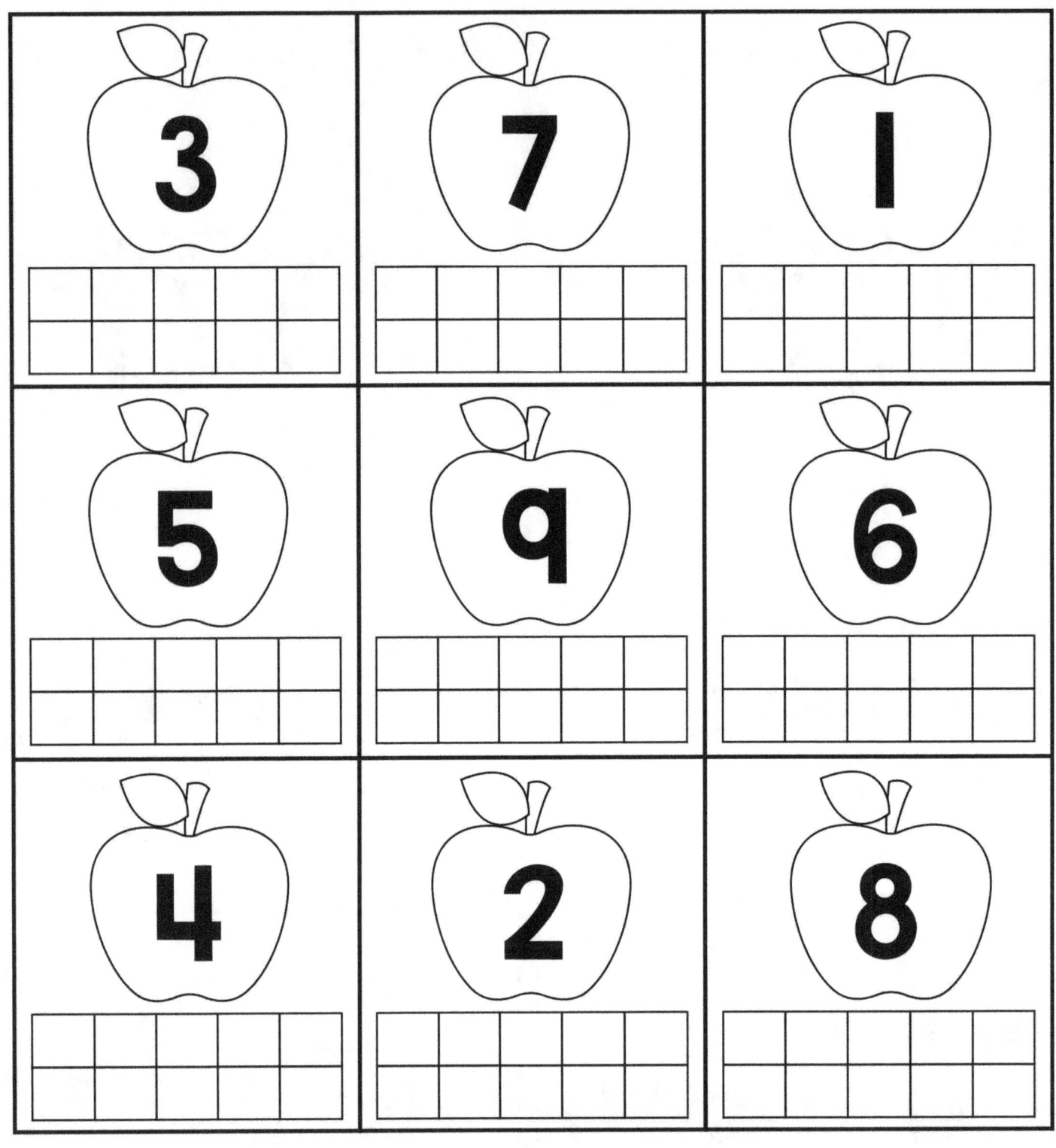

Cut And Glue The Apple

Cut and paste the part of apple in the correct place.

How Many Apples

Connect and write the answer in the boxes given below.

Left	Up	Right	Down

Cut And Glue The Apple

Cut and paste the part of apple in the correct place

Find The Apple

Find and color the path to help worm reach the apple.

Counting Apples On The Tree

Count the apples on the tree and cicle the right answer.

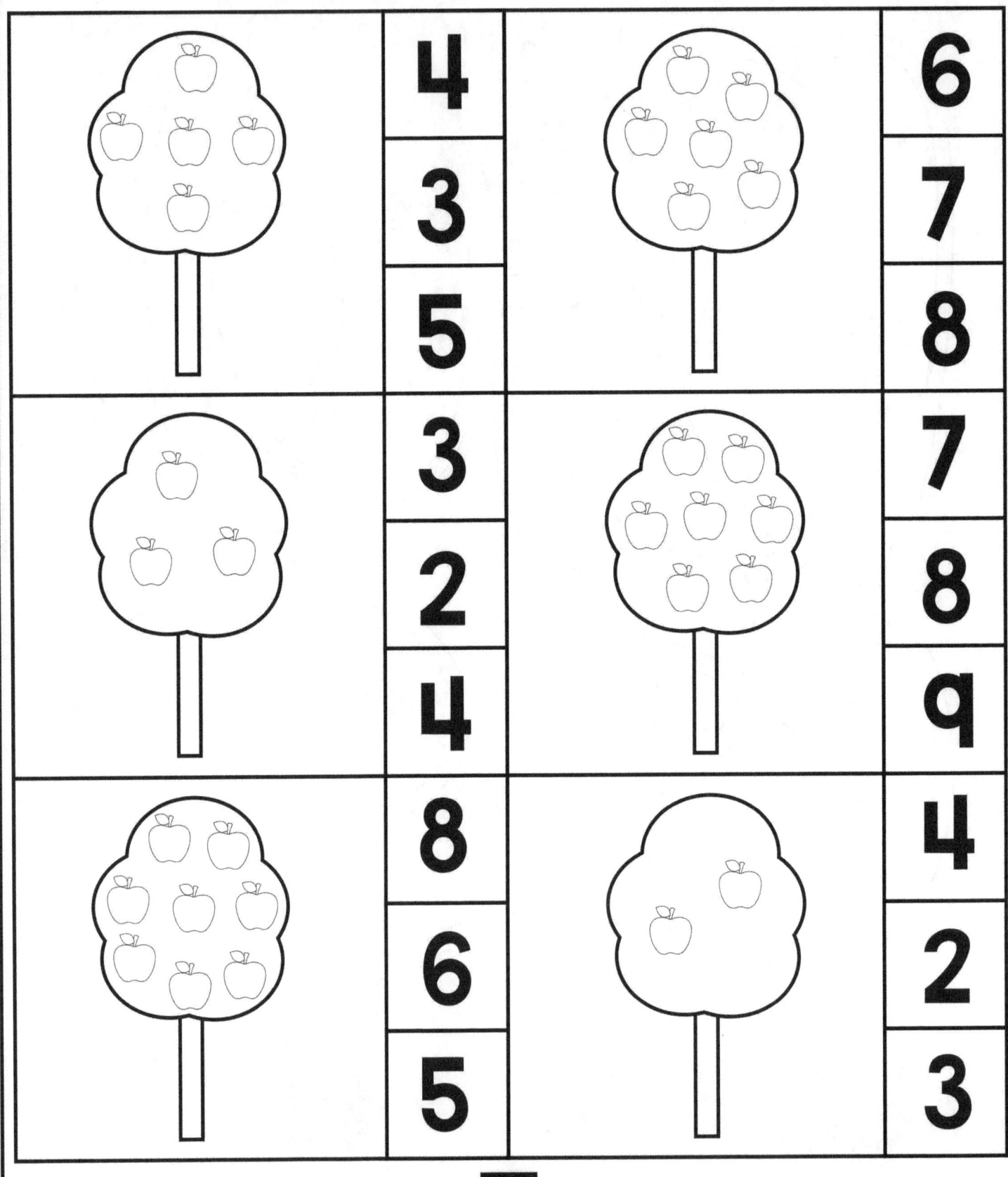

Find The Same Direction Apple

Find and connect the same direction apples.

Complete The Apple

Trace the lines to complete the apple and color it.

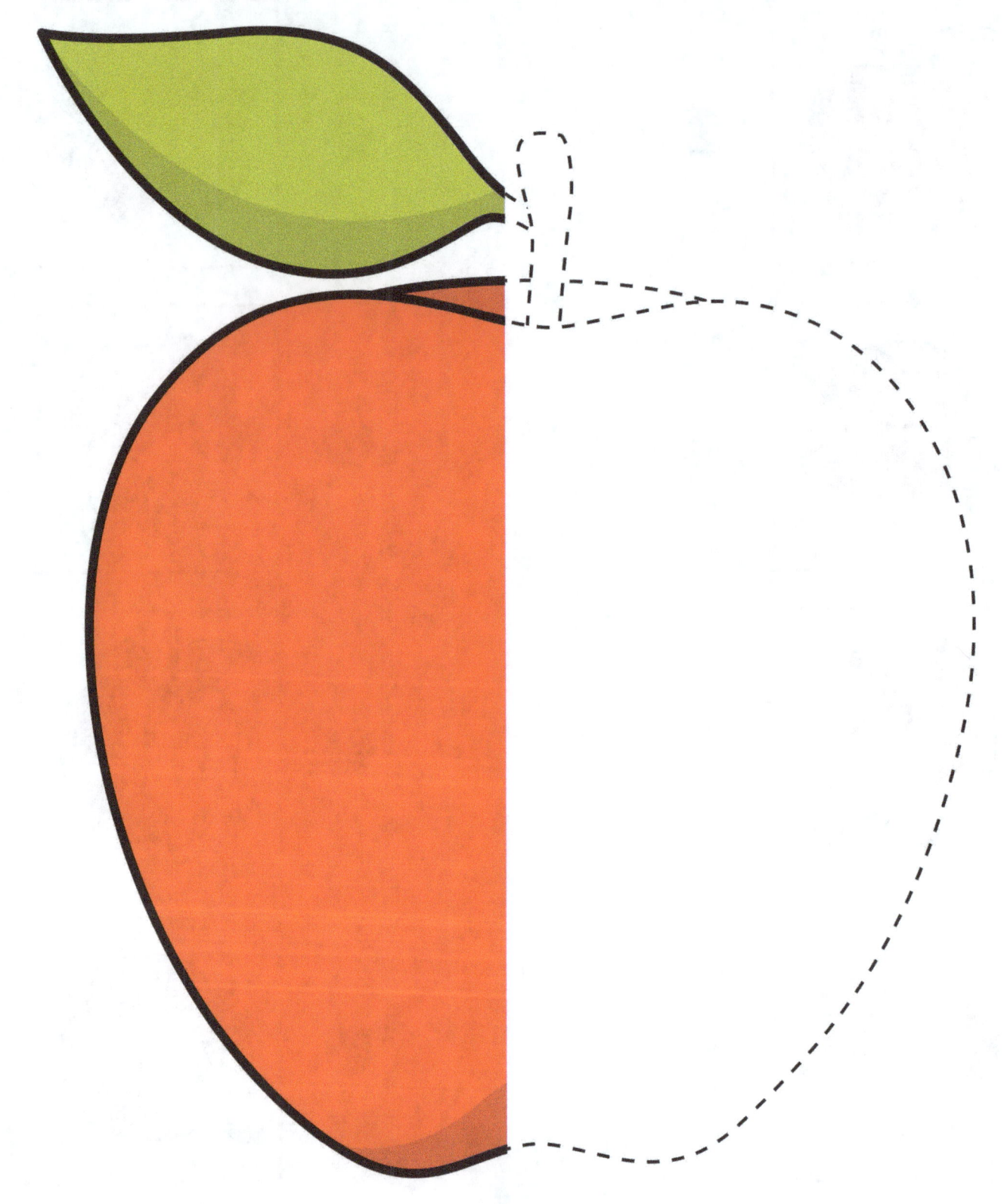

Find The Apple

Help the worm to reach the apple.

Cut And Glue

Cut and paste the parts together to complete the apple.

www.ingramcontent.com/pod-product-compliance
Lightning Source LLC
Chambersburg PA
CBHW060429010526
44118CB00017B/2428